LYING

IN THE RIVER'S

DARK BED

MADE IN MICHIGAN WRITERS SERIES

GENERAL EDITORS

Michael Delp, Interlochen Center for the Arts

M. L. Liebler, Wayne State University

ADVISORY EDITORS

Melba Joyce Boyd, *Wayne State University*

Stuart Dybek, *Western Michigan University*

Kathleen Glynn

Jerry Herron, *Wayne State University*

Laura Kasischke, *University of Michigan*

Thomas Lynch

Frank Rashid, *Marygrove College*

Doug Stanton

Keith Taylor, *University of Michigan*

A complete listing of the books in this series
can be found online at wsupress.wayne.edu

LYING

The Confluence of

IN THE RIVER'S

the Deadman and

DARK BED

the Mad Angler

POEMS BY MICHAEL DELP

Wayne State University Press
Detroit

Manufactured in the United States of America.

20 19 18 17 16   5 4 3 2 1

ISBN 978-0-8143-4198-8 (paperback)
ISBN 978-0-8143-4199-5 (e-book)

Library of Congress Control Number: 2015948595

∞

Some of the Mad Angler poems have appeared in the *Dunes Review*, *The Last Good Water*, *Outside* magazine online, *Back Country Journal*, and *Madness and Magic*. The Mad Angler poems have also been produced in a limited-edition, hand-printed chapbook from Deepwood Press. The Deadman poems have appeared in several versions as a privately published chapbook and were also printed by Talent House Press and The Ludington Writers Cooperative.

Publication of this book was made possible by a generous gift from The Meijer Foundation. Additional support was provided by Michigan Council for Arts and Cultural Affairs and National Endowment for the Arts.

Designed and typeset by Bryce Schimanski
Composed in Adobe Caslon Pro and Trade Gothic

CONTENTS

THE DEADMAN

CONFLUENCE

LYING

IN THE RIVER'S

DARK BED

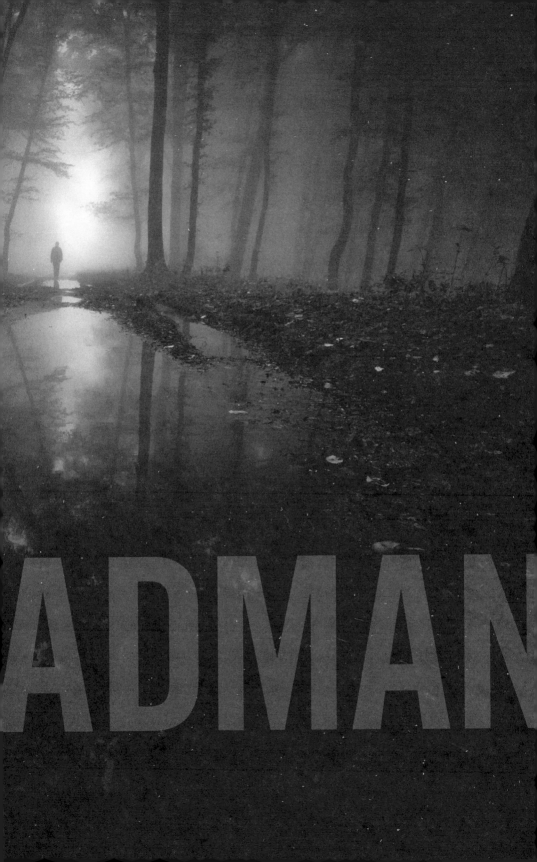

THE DEADMAN GHAZALS

1

He watches the darkness walk out of the river
and slide under his skin.
In his veins, he mistakes it for wine.

The Deadman walks the river at night,
running his hands underwater.
This is sleep, he says, his tongue's cartography
old and worn.

Sometimes you see him up in the trees, his arms like wings.
He is the crow flying at night, the dark bird entering your thighs.
Deadman dances the moon out of the sky,
the sun, the stars.
All summer he lets his body wander by itself in the
dark bed of the river.

Over a small fire, he burns his tongue, sifts his ashes,
calls himself a fire poet, smoke poet, leaves his bones dreaming in the
    embers.

2

Oh, Deadman, the moons you seek are no longer in the sky.
Look inside your heart where they are shrinking as you read.
I gave my heart away for ten buckets of river water, he replies,
and tonight I dream them running down my naked back.
Another kind of moon lost somewhere inside her thighs.
My fingers seek her wondrous heat, the real moon just now rising.

Twenty years ago I mortgaged my tongue, nailed it to the cabin door.
Tonight, the Deadman comes home, rips it down, and breathes again.

What you give away, he says, you can take back. I give this, I want to say,
offering my life, taken back again and again.

3

The wind comes up, runs down the spine of the river. He is on the bank,
cutting down small fruits of darkness.
Up on the ridges, coyotes lick the backs of shadows. The Deadman feels
his guard hairs bristle, a new country forming in his head.
He builds an altar, the dry bones of winter-kill deer, then lights a fire,
his hands sliding in, becoming the embers of a river god.
I have seen him always by himself, the Deadman alive, but not, walk-
ing upriver, the river cleaving, each stone a bright coal.

4

The Deadman sends his books down the river, one by one they slip away,
each word turning wild.
For weeks he denies the power of human language, instead, talks the
talk of bark, willow,
the hard tongue of ironwood.
Six crows scrape the yard, pick up his shadow, and for an instant there
is a dark flag in the sky, then, only dust.
He knows the correct angle of the dance in his legs when he will
suddenly turn from man to crow then, to the prophet of rivers.
What he says is unspeakable. He wants no followers. No Bible,
only the haunted memory of the one tree where he has nailed his
rabid skin.

5

There are no days in the week, no months, only the slow seepage of the
Deadman's ideas.
In the dark ribbon of sleep, he moves through swamps,
thoughts falling like invisible trail markers.
He knows those who try to follow are already lost. He loses himself.
Turns in all directions, drives his mind into the ground like a stake.
He knows exactly where he is, and finds himself looking up, into a sky
filled with black clouds, his dry skin praying for the poetry of rain.

DEADMAN MEETS JOHN WAYNE

First, Deadman tells him
his boots suck, that he's a wimp,
can't ride.
Then, Deadman gets nasty.

Deadman walks up to him,
grabs his chest hair,
breathes a little smoke into his face,
tells him his ghost has been running
the neighborhood
like a mad dog,
has bitten small children,
and Deadman stares down into John Wayne's face,
turns his eyes into the barrels of a Colt .45, says,
"The next time you see these eyes,
they'll split you up,
let some air outta' your chest.
And two holes coming out of your back.
That'll be my brand."

DEADMAN GOES HUNTING

He uses his hands,
believes in the religion of snapped necks,
holds each rabbit to his lips
before he slams them home,
then walks to his house
drunk on the kill,
drunk on the smell of death,
drunk on the way he thinks someone else,
maybe God,
must be preparing to lift him up
out of the room by his ears.
Deadman breathing the breath of God
just before his spine submerges,
goes down into his black ocean.

DEADMAN GOES BOWLING

He wanders up, staring down
what he believes is a long, thin
alley of starlight,
then takes off his head,
slips three fingers into his eyes and mouth,
and there, cradled above the floor,
he rolls his head back and forth.
On the way down
he feels like there is no such thing as wind,
imagines the pins exploding in his throat,
how each one opens into a black parachute,
drifting toward the surface of a dead planet.

DEADMAN GETS MARRIED

The night before the wedding
Deadman sleeps in his closet.
His sleep resembles the texture of rust,
or the surface of a headstone washed by shadow.

In the morning he sends a message to his bride,
decides instead to commit suicide, slowly,
sends her the tip of one of his little fingers,
that first piece of himself.

DEADMAN GOES ON VACATION

Looking at the maps,
Deadman begins to think
he could fly on top of them,
open his arms and drop in,
crashing somewhere in New Guinea,
wait there for his wife and children
to find him forty years later,
his skull perfectly preserved,
still a trace of skin
stretched over his smile.

DEADMAN'S DAUGHTER

In his hands her waist moves
like a snake through tall grass.
He sees a half moon rising
in each of her eyes,
feels the way she tries to pull
the little pools of death water
out of the pockets of sorrow
in his cheekbones.

Deadman wants to reach down
into the bucket of his stomach,
give his daughter something small and cool,
perhaps a stone to hold in her fingers,
hoping she might see strange markings
on its surface,
perhaps the directions
to bring him back to life.

TWILIGHT ZONE DEADMAN

Deadman hurts.
He hurts inside and
his skin wants to fly off
like a sheet,
warm and dry on one side,
but wet and moist on the other,
so that if you run into it,
the sheet will wrap itself around you,
and you will have the Deadman's mouth on yours,
the mask of the Deadman on your face.

Your skin will want to fly with his,
rising just above your bodies,
fusing together,
and the dance of your two skins
will be called the Deadman's Shuffle.

"TURN ME ON, DEADMAN"

Deadman's wife turns to stone,
so he sleeps closer,
runs his hand between her cold legs,
begins a slow rhythm,
which is like the power of a glacier
urging rocks up out of the earth.

Her skin ripples, just once,
then she falls asleep with him.
Pushed together, they look like
the oldest stones on earth.
Deadman dreaming the pebbles of his testicles
burning with ancient fire.

DEADMAN AS PRESIDENT

There is a new war every day.
Deadman sends everyone;
babies, old women,
even the half dead are thrown in.

Every day Deadman goes to airports
to count the bodies.
He never eats or sleeps,
but lives as though
this counting were a form of food.

Finally, no one but Deadman is left.
The stacks of bodies blot out the sun.
Deadman loves this kind of darkness,
loves to lie down in the canyons
formed by the dead
to watch the sky
blacken with vultures,
their screech becoming the Deadman's Anthem.

DEADMAN'S RELIGION

He buys a new suit,
goes on TV,
speaks with a Texas drawl,
puts his hands on the camera,
asks the women at home to move closer,
put their breasts to their screens,
all of them unaware
that Deadman has learned to turn his body
into electricity:
Deadman's tongue arcing blue fire
drifts like air into the housewives
of America.
Each home becomes an altar,
women kneeling by the thousands.
Deadman jams the voltage past infinity,
and billions of tiny hairs stand erect,
aimed like tiny rockets
at the black space of his eyes.

DEADMAN AS A WOMAN

To Deadman, breasts speak
to the inner body.
He stares into the mirror
minus his male organs,
leans close,
puts his nipples up to their reflection,
his breath fogging over his woman's face.
His fingers trace:

I love me.
I love me.
I love me.

DEADMAN AS ROCK STAR

His is the music of broken bones,
charred flesh,
the voice of an evangelist gone maniac.
Deadman uses his guitar like a cattle prod
charged with lightning.
He stands on the edge of the stage,
turns up a hundred amps
churning their eyes to liquid,
the entire audience going up in smoke,
a smell Deadman seals in his nostrils.
Later, backstage, Deadman listens in silence,
for the sound of souls
walking back through the aisles,
all of them looking to have their spirit bodies
melted down into the small, black amulets
Deadman plays with like change in his pockets.

DEADMAN OVER DETROIT

He's been circling for years,
in a slow holding pattern,
no desire to land,
just the daily, lazy turns over the suburbs,
rising and falling toward Hamtramck, River Rouge, Inkster, then back
    up again,
his heart fueled by leftover car parts, exhaust fumes drifting out of
    abandoned auto plants.
Each pass and his belly fills with rusted engines, broken glass, the
    bricks of abandoned houses.
Sometimes at night, over the ghost of Briggs Stadium,
he dreams the city back to how it was . . .
lost neighborhoods rise up out of the charred dust,
he sees Milt Plum and Bobby Layne connecting again,
Gil Hodges sprints back to life,
sifting under Deadman's shadow as if it were a pop fly,
his glove waving in the air,
the sign to bring Deadman on home.

DEADMAN'S DOG DREAM

His first dream memory: junkyard dogs,
how he slid up to them,
licked their wounds,
let that oil blood in their hearts
drip into his veins,
his lips turning an angry, bruise-blue yellow,
so that when he rose up to the day
he would turn on you at any moment,
and whisper into both of your ears at the same time,

"These teeth can bite through metal
turn flesh purple instantly,
and most likely
they will rip to shreds,
that leash your body
has clipped to your soul."

DEADMAN'S MYTH

for Norm Wheeler

Deadman, Deadman,
you got no bones.
Deadman, Deadman,
you look so old.

And then Deadman walks up to you,
ice-blue eyes
made of wind from the Arctic Circle.
and that old Norse Beast of Dreams story,
beating on the door of your face,
singing:

"Living man, living man,
let me in."

DEADMAN'S SORROW

From the shin bone of his right leg,
Deadman dreams of making a flute,
writing a song which mimics the low howl
slipping between his clenched teeth.

Dancing a death jig on one leg,
his arms flailing in the wind,
Deadman wants to dance long enough
to dissolve himself into the ground,
underground if he can,
so that he might lift the dead into his arms,
carve their bones into wind instruments.
Imagines how he might teach the dead to play,
so that at night, before the living fell asleep,
they would hear the sound of air moving
through the bones of their beloved,
Deadman conducting the only song he knows:
a lullaby,
the notes drifting off like birds to die
in the night air.

DEADMAN IN VIETNAM

Deadman moves through the jungle
like a giant knife in the wind.
Out ahead he sees brown faces,
bodies rise up,
and he mows them to stubble.
At night he dreams a giant hand
is shaving all the hair from his body.
In the morning he hears his scalp
being nailed over the giant's door,
then blades moving toward him,
a battalion of choppers coming in low,
upside down, their rotors whispering:
"Deadman, Deadman,
run toward home."

PROFESSOR DEADMAN

For a while, Deadman plays it straight,
reads the classics,
memorizes Shakespeare,
can call up every allusion in Pound,
knows the meaning of Eliot's epigrams,
can explain the mystery of Poetry.

Then, he begins to go insane,
comes to believe that the study of English
is a form of terrorism.
He stalks the campus with a slang gun,
taking potshots at his colleagues,
shoots the correct usage out of their mouths,
gets the guys with PhDs to say,
"Them are nice pants."

At the English department meeting
they call him in.
"I ain't late, is me," he says.
They move to censure him,
ask for his credentials,
tell him to turn in his office copies of
The Elements Of Style.

"It don't matter to me," he says.
"Me got a new language.
It work like this,
Everything the Deadman
say is a new part of speech."

For weeks Deadman hunts down vocabulary words,
nails them like skins to his office door,
gets his students to use one-syllable words,
guttural sounds, double negatives,

dangling participles,
assigns essays
using only sentence fragments,
has all of them believing that Standard English
is like a strange virus able to rot their tongues,
that his PhD is really in Pharmacy
and he has the cure.

DEADMAN FANTASY

He wants the fattest lip,
the largest thigh,
the biggest woman he can conjure
out of his dreams,
wants her to smother him,
surround his tiny body
so that he might turn himself
into a single point,
fall into her, through her,
come out the other side,
with enough breath in him to sing,
"Bring me a year of nights,
bring me enough darkness to make her last."

DEADMAN TEACHES

To Deadman the blackboard is like space,
and instead of writing on the surface,
he turns his back on the class,
jumps in, his arms flailing,
drifting away from the room,
as the students wander up to the board,
trying to call him back,
their eyes blistering
from Deadman's heat,
Deadman flaring into a supernova,
blazing Deadman alone in the sky,
his students dreaming they breathe the smoke
old Deadman stars.

HORMONE DEADMAN

At the rest home for boring adults
Deadman sets up a hormone machine,
suctions their testosterone and estrogen
into gallon jugs, then sets up a spa for himself:
a hot tub boiling with adolescent juices.

After weeks of treatment, Deadman feels 16 again.
High on hormones,
he prowls the wasteland for bodies,
dragging burnt-out teachers to his machine.

Months pass.
Deadman becomes the Hulk of hormones.
His body is one living hormonal tissue.
More than a madman,
he feels every day like he did
when he made love for the first time,
that his body is somehow electric,
full of surges,
his brain full of lightning,
the world offering itself for burning.

MEETING DEADMAN

They make a mistake,
make him chairman,
and Deadman uses the rules of order
like miniature whips,
beats down each question,
flogs the vice chairman into submission.

At each meeting he says,
we will have another meeting,
which will, in turn, have a meeting of its own.
We will meet constantly.
Our lives will become meetings.
We will write memos to each other
about the content of all meetings.
At the beginning of each meeting we will chant
the word meeting until we reach a consensus.
We will form a meeting committee
with a subcommittee to discuss meetings.

All day, all night, Deadman meets.
He begins to believe everything in life
should be run by meetings.
To have a baby, you must have a meeting.
There are death meetings, sleep meetings,
meetings for divorces and meetings
for appendectomies.

Deadman becomes the Billy Graham of meetings.
He writes a meeting Bible, gets a meeting network,
which broadcasts only meetings.
He asks for money to have meetings, then sets up meetings to have
    meetings

about meeting for money.
Finally, he can find no one left to meet with
who is not already in a meeting,
so he watches videos of meetings,
runs them slow, runs them fast-forward,
watches himself gavel off heads like golf balls,
turns the phrase "killer meeting" into the gospel.

ANONYMOUS DEADMAN

Deadman wants to be utterly unknown,
wants to be like the dust
between the bones of the dead.
He wants no phone number,
no social security digits,
wants to have his name removed
from all lists,
his number eradicated from every computer.
He wants to live alone at the end of a dark,
impassable road,
and fall asleep every night knowing
no one will ever see him again.
And he wants to rise up every day
like a missing person,
all his mail, marked, "Deceased."

SIXTEEN DEADMAN

for Rod Goldfarb

From inside himself, Deadman watches
his organs baste in hormonal stew.
He knows his girlfriend is sending him signals,
knows she dreams of a Harley or a Triumph
without a chain guard,
some wild piece of steel
ripping through soft fog.

At night, after a date,
Deadman listens to himself cooling down,
the quiet snap of a piston getting smaller,
those tiny filaments in his headlight
still glowing,
the sound of oil dripping slowly into the pan,
his throttle still warm from a night of riding.

ACCOUNTANT DEADMAN

Deadman puts on a gray suit,
gets a haircut.
Each day he memorizes
the stock pages of the *Wall Street Journal.*
He begins to use phrases like "capital gain," "disbursement of funds,"
    "net gain,"
"gross receipts," thinks of himself as the poet of money.
Deadman begins eating money.
First he chews dollar bills,
then tries them in salads,
each day a new dish,
a soufflé of fifties,
twenty-dollar casseroles,
the oval centers of Ben Franklins for dessert.

Each day he shuffles to his underground office,
marks his arrival in the credit column,
then lies down on his sofa,
calls his secretary in,
tells her about his money fetish,
how he has made underwear out of stock certificates,
then slips on his rubber thumb guards,
lays her on the desk, flips through her clothes
as if they were new bills.

ELECTROSHOCK DEADMAN

Outside on a snowy day,
Deadman is starting his car,
gets a brainstorm
and hooks the jumpers to his head.

Electric drugs,
the synapses turning to syrup,
the visions Deadman sees:

Every woman he ever loved
melting into one form,
the fangs hidden just under two
pouting lips,
breasts luminous under a cotton dress, her arms waving
in the current of his electricity.

He wanders the woods for days,
hallucinating the words he always intended to say,
in love poems,
his skin charred,
dragging behind him like a shadow.

VOODOO DEADMAN

He moves into a huge basement,
covers the small windows with black nylon,
then begins to carve the bones of his legs
into pins.
He spends months making perfect replicas
of his enemies,
swats them around like slaves,
pays particular attention to their eyes,
wants to look in when he sends in a pin.
He reads the local paper every night,
speaks the obituaries like poems,
then lies down in his bed of dolls,
brings their lips to his,
mouths the curses of the dead as if they were
lullabies.

It takes months to drop them all.
Deadman without enemies,
stalking the corridors inside his body
trying to push the knives out of his back.

ART DEADMAN

For years it's the same game:
paint another landscape,
write another poem,
erect another sculpture from cow skulls,
Deadman doing his art,
all blacks,
the deep blue of bruises.

He longs for his own gallery,
concocts a plan to enter the head
of every living person,
use his acrylic blood as paint,
each human being reeling
from Deadman thrusting like Pollock
against the dark inner canvases of their skulls.

DEADMAN AS WRITER

Deadman treats words like road kill,
runs them down, stops,
rolls backward and forward,
over and over.
After he flattens thousands of words,
he thinks he has invented a new language.
He writes a book,
says,
"Here, read this,
it will kill you."

CONFLUENCE

They meet in a waking dream, fading daylight, a low sun coming in. The Deadman has floated downriver and come upon the Mad Angler, bent over a smoldering fire. They know they have known each other for centuries. "Read to me," the Angler says, and the Deadman pours out his poems like so much water, emptying himself. While the Deadman reads and pours, the Mad Angler fills himself up. If you saw this, you would think that the Deadman was weeping directly into the Mad Angler's head. This is like that South American ritual where the shaman touches his eyeball to yours and suddenly knows your life back beyond your birth. Together, they stand with their backs to the sun, watch their shadows step out well away from the ground and merge, the Angler chanting his own poems back into the Deadman, who rests on the edge of the fire, his voice, hot and deep, bouncing off the rising thermal. They both know they have the oldest lessons you can carry, and they also know their lives have fused deeply enough to make of the world a cauldron of purely distilled desire, that sacred place where they will drink beyond the barrier of time and death, their merged shadows vanishing into the darkening woods.

DEADMAN/MAD ANGLER SINGING UP THE COUNTRY

They load their ancient Power Wagon with small gods, tiny bellies, but protruding. They crush together in the pickup bed and point the way to the backcountry. In the rearview mirror they bounce like bobbleheads in the dust. Once there, they pick a worthless spot of land, all scrub oak and washouts, red sumac wild as far as they can see. Their ancient chant starts low, then moves like a wave over the ground. The Deadman feels his skin lift like a sheet, settling over the Mad Angler, who lies in the dirt, arms outstretched, his arms aimed toward the sky. Water rises up out of his feet, washes out of his eye sockets, and the wild ones, those almost forgotten gods of creeks, and seeps, the ones who keep watch over even the smallest of springs in the woods, they ready their lines, make their casts into the eddying current. The Mad Angler becomes a vessel for what will become rain, well water, the nectar of thunderstorms.

HORMONE CISTERN

The Deadman and the Mad Angler bathe under a red moon, chanting poems back and forth, entire passages of books, whole chapters verbatim, even the Bible is sent up into the red mist. While they sing and speak, every maiden they have ever conned dances around the cistern the Deadman has filled with testosterone. They laugh and watch them smolder, these young wood and water nymphs, their bodies undulating against their skin as if they were fish. Things heat up, the cistern swirling of its own, and then one of them, the tall, cool white one, skin like mother-of-pearl, ice in her blood, that northern one with a breastplate made of ancient star debris, settles in and cools things down, water turning cooler and cooler, the poems caught in the throats of old men, until she picks them up as the frozen cubes they have become, takes them home where she will hide them in her soul freezer, takes them out on one of those full moons in January when trees explode from the cold, and throws their frozen tongues into the swirling river where she sleeps.

THE MAD ANGLER AND DEADMAN CAMPFIRE

They burn three-piece suits and wingtips. They burn syllabi and forms, anything they can find to eradicate the academic life, or the life of bankers and corporate demons. They burn maps and directions, no-trespassing signs. They burn all their certificates of merit, awards, any and all bad collections of poetry. As they burn, they sing, and as they sing, they become characters in songs. "Ol' Man River" falls down and out of the air and collapses by the embers, and every song ever written and played by they Grateful Dead rises up out of the dark into a black plume miles high. Together they both grow wings, one insect, the other vulture, and they ride and circle the black swirling vein of debris they have made of their burning. In the morning, bottles empty for hundreds of yards, they rise to step into the new shadows of the legends they have made of themselves.

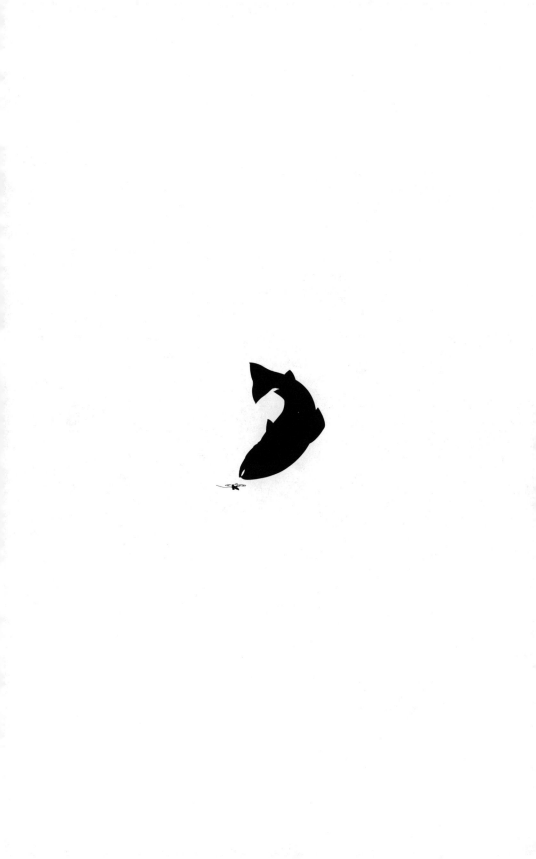

THE MAD ANGLER AND DEADMAN CAMPFIRE

They burn three-piece suits and wingtips. They burn syllabi and forms, anything they can find to eradicate the academic life, or the life of bankers and corporate demons. They burn maps and directions, no-trespassing signs. They burn all their certificates of merit, awards, any and all bad collections of poetry. As they burn, they sing, and as they sing, they become characters in songs. "Ol' Man River" falls down and out of the air and collapses by the embers, and every song ever written and played by they Grateful Dead rises up out of the dark into a black plume miles high. Together they both grow wings, one insect, the other vulture, and they ride and circle the black swirling vein of debris they have made of their burning. In the morning, bottles empty for hundreds of yards, they rise to step into the new shadows of the legends they have made of themselves.

HORMONE CISTERN

The Deadman and the Mad Angler bathe under a red moon, chanting poems back and forth, entire passages of books, whole chapters verbatim, even the Bible is sent up into the red mist. While they sing and speak, every maiden they have ever conned dances around the cistern the Deadman has filled with testosterone. They laugh and watch them smolder, these young wood and water nymphs, their bodies undulating against their skin as if they were fish. Things heat up, the cistern swirling of its own, and then one of them, the tall, cool white one, skin like mother-of-pearl, ice in her blood, that northern one with a breastplate made of ancient star debris, settles in and cools things down, water turning cooler and cooler, the poems caught in the throats of old men, until she picks them up as the frozen cubes they have become, takes them home where she will hide them in her soul freezer, takes them out on one of those full moons in January when trees explode from the cold, and throws their frozen tongues into the swirling river where she sleeps.

DEADMAN/MAD ANGLER SINGING UP THE COUNTRY

They load their ancient Power Wagon with small gods, tiny bellies, but protruding. They crush together in the pickup bed and point the way to the backcountry. In the rearview mirror they bounce like bobbleheads in the dust. Once there, they pick a worthless spot of land, all scrub oak and washouts, red sumac wild as far as they can see. Their ancient chant starts low, then moves like a wave over the ground. The Deadman feels his skin lift like a sheet, settling over the Mad Angler, who lies in the dirt, arms outstretched, his arms aimed toward the sky. Water rises up out of his feet, washes out of his eye sockets, and the wild ones, those almost forgotten gods of creeks, and seeps, the ones who keep watch over even the smallest of springs in the woods, they ready their lines, make their casts into the eddying current. The Mad Angler becomes a vessel for what will become rain, well water, the nectar of thunderstorms.

CONFLUENCE

They meet in a waking dream, fading daylight, a low sun coming in. The Deadman has floated downriver and come upon the Mad Angler, bent over a smoldering fire. They know they have known each other for centuries. "Read to me," the Angler says, and the Deadman pours out his poems like so much water, emptying himself. While the Deadman reads and pours, the Mad Angler fills himself up. If you saw this, you would think that the Deadman was weeping directly into the Mad Angler's head. This is like that South American ritual where the shaman touches his eyeball to yours and suddenly knows your life back beyond your birth. Together, they stand with their backs to the sun, watch their shadows step out well away from the ground and merge, the Angler chanting his own poems back into the Deadman, who rests on the edge of the fire, his voice, hot and deep, bouncing off the rising thermal. They both know they have the oldest lessons you can carry, and they also know their lives have fused deeply enough to make of the world a cauldron of purely distilled desire, that sacred place where they will drink beyond the barrier of time and death, their merged shadows vanishing into the darkening woods.

THE MAD ANGLER'S WATER GOSPEL

Meditate on this: your own skin washed for days in the river as one
    might wash a bed sheet,
then hung to dry in the sun, left overnight to soak up the mist
coming off the water, dried again in the sun and decorated with fish
    paintings
rendered in your own blood.
Imagine it now, furling and unfurling in a July breeze,
riding the air like a prayer flag.
Stepping close, pressing it to your face
you would smell again the deep, abiding scent of cedar.

Meditate on this also: to ever wear this skin again is to say that water
is in the bucket that fuels the soul,
that to wear this skin is to pray
that your skin could become loosed from itself
that it might seek lower ground,
places to gather itself
before vanishing into the sky.

THE MAD ANGLER BORN AGAIN

It comes in summer, maybe late June,
a night filled with moonlight,
the marrow pull of moon-path, the constant thrum in his blood
telling him he has an emptiness which must be filled.
He walks to the river to make amends,
seeking atonement for the sins
of fishing with bait as a child,
the souls of countless bass and bluegills
haunting the edges of his dreams.
He comes to get right with all the gods of water,
those invisible ones who guard every bend,
always whispering in his ear about bad casts,
their oft-ignored warnings about hungry maidens
in dark waters.
Where this happens is a cathedral of cedars vaulted into the sky,
a congregation of insects, and riffles.
This mad one stands in full current, bends low,
spreads out his hands, reads the scripture of water.
Something in his head breaks loose,
swirls, comes up out of the milky light of the moon,
sees the world as it was meant to be:
water, reflected light, mile after mile of the river's blood moving
        through him,
all those maidens shedding their lovely, translucent skins.

THE MAD ANGLER SPEAKS TRUTH TO POWER

I say that water is better than money,
something wet and smooth to be taken in, coveted.
I say that long ago, we spoke to water and it spoke back.
Water is a form of being saved,
lying down, seeking something wise in our cells,
looking for gradients,
places to run and places to rest.
I claim that once in a dream
I walked on water.
Storms came.
I entered the clouds and when I came back down,
I spit the truth.

You might know this truth in your own ears,
when sleep fails and you walk out in half moonlight,
listening for crows gathering darkness into their throats,
knowing you have lost track of the river:
They tell you the way, upstream,
crow talk, how water finds its own way,
summons you as a kind of reservoir,
giving you more knowing than you ever thought possible
in case you ever become lost again.

THE MAD ANGLER IN THE CATHEDRAL

He spends a year removing the vaulted roof
fueled by the desire
to look up at night into a sanctuary of stars.
When he works, he speaks the names of ghosts,
the liturgy of entomology embedded
in the dark water of his brain.
He believes in the gospel of intricate casts,
the psalm of mending line,
and drinking from the baptismal font,
he prays that all the angels of rivers might drift down,
the sound of hymns replaced by the singing of fly lines
they cast over the heads of bait fishermen.
In the end he tears down the walls,
channels a river through the pews,
and waits in the rain for the wild god of trout
to turn each swimming miracle
loose from his hands.

THE EPIPHANY OF THE MAD ANGLER

When they called for my intellect I told them
it was dead,
buried at the end of some worthless two-track
with a box of textbooks,
then I walked to the river to live among the fish,
and when they asked for my instincts
I told them I made a trade for the sense
that rides on the surface of the river.
I knew instantly that sense when I learned the water of rivers
collects and eddies not in pools,
but in dark pockets of wisdom,
places under sweeping cedars
where river stones have arranged themselves
into messages,
a kind of Braille,
places where the tongue of a man
wants to slide out of his head,
swim away.

THE MAD ANGLER'S RESTITUTION

Already the swamps have dried up, each day becomes more like a desert
than some flowing heart.
He swears off rivers,
begins the slow process of unlearning the bends he loves,
loses track of his favorite runs and pools where
he has cashed in his precious time.
The rods go up in flames,
the sweet smell of bamboo mixing with resin,
the dust and blood of boyhood creels.
He speaks into an overcast sky,
asking what it will take to make up for all the times
he thought he knew what he was doing:
the arrogance of admiring perfect casts,
forgetting to slip brook trout easily back into the river's seams,
how his body and mind bent to the shape
of each day on the water.
All of it taken for granted: his laughter under dark cedars,
sweet cigars, his beating heart,
even the moon.

ADVICE OF THE MAD ANGLER

1

If you are miles from a river,
and you hear moving water,
have the sense to follow the woman next to you,
out the door, into the woods,
where her body will surround you,
that pure current of her flesh,
smoothing you into that dark river stone
she might carry in her pocket.

2

Find the dream where you stand
in the confluence of all the rivers you have ever fished.
Renounce ambition and embrace
that ragged dog of the river you have become.

Drink snowmelt, springwater,
spend your life seeking
that one bourbon spilling from the mouth
of a woman who can make the sound of a river
in your ear.

Make this pact: think of fishing as gathering soul money,
trade the job for the current,
any meeting for a long riffle,
make of your life a tapestry of casts
woven into something another man
would pronounce legend.
Obey your inner tides.
Find the truth
written on the skins of brook trout.

THE MAD ANGLER REVEALS HIS OTHER SPIRIT ANIMAL

Thirty years ago a wolverine crawled into my heart
and has stayed there all these years.
He eats snow and chunks of ice,
the bitter flesh of failure
I pass down to him like breadcrumbs.
It's almost as if he is living under the front porch.
He watches everything, and at night I hear him
cough up his dreams.
He wants to go out in the yard
but attacks everything that moves,
so I keep him lodged in close, no leash, no rope, no collar.
He loves it inside me, claims there is a certain mist in my heart
which he prefers to sunlight.
I would have given him a name long ago,
but he says he doesn't need one.
He sniffs the air and tells me what's coming
to dismantle me.
he circles like a dog before he sleeps,
but when I reach to pet him, there's nothing there,
but coarse hair, wrapped around a muscle
beating itself to death.

THE PRAYER OF THE MAD ANGLER

I pray that the water in the heart of Buddha might enter the bedrooms
of politicians and sweep them out of their doors, into the drainage
ditches we have dug behind their houses.

I pray that the water in the heart of Jesus might wash away the sins of
fools who erect dams, channel rivers, build levees, and create false
cataracts in the lobbies of hotels.

I pray for eddies, backwaters, the slow places where current cannot find
its way,

and I pray for shallow riffles where gravel churns up new words
constantly,

the river a book spoken in all kinds of weather.

I pray to the individual gods of feeder creeks and seeps and the smallest
gods

of single dew drops slipping each morning into the river.

I pray that I might go to the river and lie down, that I might open my
mouth and feel

a thousand cubic feet per second cleanse me like a sluice.

I pray that the road into the secret river places might disappear, that I
might one day enter the river and vanish into the silver reflection
of the sky.

a new talisman against the dark heart of developers,
the pavers and city planners,
those feral hogs of greed who eat what's left of old rivers,
and what used to be acres of wetlands, their bellies filled
with dollar bills and the piss-swill of corporate runoff.

3

You pray for a second coming, the sky to open,
for people to be carried off, raptured.
I pray each morning for entire counties to vanish,
the boardrooms of Big Water and Big Oil to warp out of existence,
cities to suddenly evaporate, forest to come back and parking lots
to suddenly turn back to pasture.
I pray for the engines of fracking to break down,
their lines filled with sand and the sludge of money,
but the deepest prayer seeks more rivers, more flow,
hydrology as a new religion,
the study of glacial till as sacred as the Bible.
I ask for the lords of each river to band together,
find the secret map where the one God has his hands
on the floodgate,
his fingers itching to do some new miracles.

THE PSALMS OF THE MAD ANGLER

1

This daily summer ritual:
walking up toward the ridge in the middle
of a feeder creek,
stopping at the pool just below the rock ledge,
dipping first my hands and then my head,
my ears burning with the sound of roiled water.
My scalp numbs, then my eyes,
and if only for an instant, I retrieve my savage name:
He-Who-Sees-as-a-River.
Working my way back to the cabin,
half-blind,
I feel my way through the trees.
My feet know the way through deadfall,
and those wild crows overhead ...
they chant the way to the door.

2

In the dreamtime, millennia ago,
the aboriginal ancestors in Australia sang up the country,
literally walked the land and sang it into being.
Last night a bird from one of those ancient songs
fell into my sleep and left a path
through the air,
changed my tongue and heart into a language I knew
had been carried down through my DNA and I went to work,
walked in to the middle of the woods,
sang a river into my arms,
then followed it downhill, knowing it would disappear into where it
        came from,
sinking into my heart tissue, rising up daily as I need it,

THE MAD ANGLER SPEAKS TRUTH TO POLITICIANS

Over 65 years ago, as soon as I could walk,
I abandoned myself to water.
I prowled lakes and creeks, rivers and swamps.
Now, I sit on the edge of the woods
where river meets sky and I tell you this:
As surely as water is blood,
as surely as my blood is water,
what you have done over decades of greed
has turned your hearts into pus pumps.
I would trade most of you for a single river.
You have done enough and your
malignant work is done.
Had I the power, I would banish you
to a nation made entirely of sand,
a black sun in a black sky, no rain,
each one of you exiled to a tiny hut
beside a river made of oil where not even
your sandy tears would make a difference.

THE MAD ANGLER'S WRITER'S MANIFESTO

Think of every poem as water.
Think of that water dammed, channeled, culverted, bottled, ditched, diverted,
and generally throttled.
Or: the elderly woman stuck in a kitchen band with saxophones lodged in her bones,
or lapdogs parked on the porch who yearn to wander the neighbors' garbage cans
suddenly turned into Great Pyrenees Mountain dogs off the leash for good,
or that vision you once had of yourself as a writer
drawn through the needle's eye of too much school, the lectures by the boring
for the bored to keep them bored and thinking that poetry
is something to cut up like a pig in a biology class,
when what you have left is only the parts and nothing of the pigness.
Think of the sky filled with stones instead of wandering clouds,
or the wings of birds made of concrete instead of mostly the air in their bones,
or think of the skin of the person you love wrapped in lovely barbed wire,
of the sun sitting in the sky as a bowling ball giving off darkness.
Then, think of that water up there in the beginning of this manifesto
suddenly turned loose, winding, meandering,
paused in a slow eddy,
then coursing, falling, into
the sweet madness of poetry itself.

sifting out of the trees.
I praise the lust for emergences,
the urge to quit the job,
convert the pension funds to river frontage,
the sudden impulse to carry a fly rod into a meeting,
the fly ripping at the lips of your superiors.
I embrace the chant of waterfalls,
the litany of holy rivers: Bitterroot, Rock Creek, Yellowstone.

I trust only the sweet smell of rotting cedar,
the scent of mudbanks festering with nymphs,
rivers rising in my blood like an illness,
a fever sent by the god of desire to make his presence known,
something jolting through the veins to replace
the done deal, the raise with the corner office,
the soul trader you most likely have become.

THE MAD ANGLER'S MANIFESTO

I speak with the voice of water,
rivulet, brook, stream, and creek,
for whitewater in lost gorges,
boiling cataracts, every place
where the souls of wild fish gather
to remind us of the power of hydrology.
I speak with the name of rain,
the soft lips of condensation,
even the dew which gathers each night,
every drop another transition from sky to earth.
I invoke masses of insects to take over the world,
to begin the hatching and mating,
sure in the fact that tomorrow
another dam will fail, another levee will crumble,
another river where you live will tire of its banks,
seek retribution on your lawn,
running up your driveway and into your basement.

I praise the flash flood,
the artesian well,
the flowing hearts under our feet,
the webs of underground rivers coursing
through solid rock.

I fish in incantations, genuflections,
my body a living mark for the crest gauge,
tidal fluctuation, flood tides and fresh water seiches.
When my eye falls on rivers, I praise their transparency,
their nature of shaping their way as they move.

Water is my heart churning in a white hydraulic,
my tongue longing for a quiet pool,
the skin of night settling in,
mayflies on the edge of moonlight

LYING

IN THE RIVER'S

DARK BED

Advance praise for

LYING IN THE RIVER'S DARK BED

"John Berryman and Patti Smith had a son, and his name was Mike Delp's poems. This book is a mysterious amplifier with '11' on the dial. Delp's Mad Angler poems want to make you sane; and the Deadman of these poems wants you to live. Read these two sections in a rush, one after another, as I did, and you make your own river in the air around the living room, or campfire. They become a prayer. You can see a god waking very suddenly in the corner, wide-eyed, just the whites of the eyes, having been asleep for years— looking around, looking around."

—Doug Stanton, *New York Times* bestselling author

"As the hip kids would say, Deadman kills it. One of the most memorable personas in contemporary Michigan literature (sorry to use the 'L' word, Deadman), Delp's trickster is at once feral and dumber than we are smart, challenging our antiquated views of how art should behave. One must harken back to the little-known but seminal Chilean poet Nicanor Parra to find a writer so deft at creating 'anti-poems' that both move the reader and revivify the poetic. Immerse yourself, reader, in this river's dark bed, then surface gasping—and more alive."

—Chris Dombrowski, author of *Earth Again*
(Wayne State University Press, 2013)

"Michael Delp is our state's poetic Intimidator/Enchanter. He intimidates with unexpected images, 'Upon the ridge, coyotes lick the backs of shadows.' And enchants with, 'Find the truth written on the skins of brook trout.' Deadman meets Mad Angler: Only Delp, only Delp. More, anon."

— Joseph Heywood, author of *The Snowfly*

Advance praise for

LYING IN THE RIVER'S DARK BED

"The poems in Mike Delp's stunning new collection must have emerged from that crack in the world between sleeping and waking. They're as raw and bloody as newborn myths, and they're howling to be heard. Listen to them. Drink them. Eat them. Then throw away your old life and start over. Delp says, 'Here, read this, it will kill you.' It will, it did."

—Jerry Dennis, author of *A Daybreak Handbook*
and *The Windward Shore*

"In the first of David's *Psalms*, the righteous man is likened to 'a tree planted by the rivers of water, that bringeth forth his fruit in his season.' Michael Delp is such a man, and these poems are the fruits of his lifelong, steadfast, deeply rooted devotion to the holy waters that nourish his wild heart: 'O taste and see . . .'"

—Nick Bozanic, author of *Lost River Fugue*